The ABCs of Adulthood

The
ABCs
of Adulthood

An Alphabet of Life Lessons

Text by Deborah Copaken

Photographs by
Deborah Copaken *and* Randy Polumbo

CHRONICLE BOOKS
SAN FRANCISCO

Library of Congress Cataloging-in-Publication Data available.

ISBN 978-1-4521-5191-5

Manufactured in China

Design by Jennifer Tolo Pierce

10 9 8 7 6 5 4

Chronicle books and gifts are available at special quantity
discounts to corporations, professional associations, literacy
programs, and other organizations. For details and discount
information, please contact our premiums department at
corporatesales@chroniclebooks.com or at 1-800-759-0190.

Chronicle Books LLC
680 Second Street
San Francisco, CA 94107
www.chroniclebooks.com

For Jacob and Sasha, better late than never;

For Nico, right on time;

And for Leo, who still has many years to go.

So. You're an adult now. Bravo! You might be heading off to college or university. Maybe you're about to embark on your first job, or you're getting ready to blow out more candles on a birthday cake than seem possible to extinguish with a single breath. Or perhaps you are in your mid-thirties, still living at home with your parents, glued to your video game console, and totally confused about how to level up.

Whatever the occasion, chances are you're holding this book in your hand because somebody cared enough about you to understand that while you've mastered your ABCs and can fry an egg with ease, you're still learning how to read subtext and sauté a life.

Well, take a seat. This book will save you. Or at the very least, it will save you a heap of confusion and rookie mistakes. I know. I made them. If someone had just given me the Y, D, A, and H in this book at the beginning of my adulthood, it could have saved me an entire M is for Mortgage's worth of therapy bills.

I actually meant to write this for my eldest before he left home. I started several months before his departure, but that deadline came and went, because B is also for

Busy when you have C is for Children. I made it to F and gave up. I also meant to make him a photo album of his entire childhood, but I had a problem accessing everything taken between 2003 and 2007. (Maybe one of you can come over and help me with that before he's handed his diploma.) I finally reached Z before my daughter left home, so at least now I can hand this to the baby of the family as I shove him out of the nest.

No seriously, I don't shove. I will push. Firmly. And then I will unplug the video game console. Forever.

A is for Anger

Anger is a totally useless emotion. You'll feel it, of course, because you're only human. Next time you do, I would urge you to become extremely present, conscious, and hyperaware of your anger. Don't judge and don't react: just notice it. Practice this enough, and you will learn to simply identify your anger, transcend it, and push it aside. A, after all, is also for another sort of individual (two syllables, ends with *hole*, you know the type). Next time you're driving and one of them cuts you off while giving you the finger, see what it feels like to simply notice that rage without returning it. You will meet a whole boatload of these types on your voyage through life. That doesn't mean you have to stoop to their level. Ever.

B is for Bed

Make yours every day, no excuses, end of story, amen.
If you think making your bed is a waste of time, that's
your prerogative. However, in a world where almost
nothing is within your control, the fact that every morn-
ing you can smooth out the creases and wrangle order
into the one tiny element of your environment—to which
you will be returning later that night—will fill you with
the kind of peace and gratitude that will serve as the
perfect counterpoise to the chaos of daily life.

C is for Children

Wait, what? Children? (You're saying to yourself right now.) *Are you kidding? I'm just getting started!* Yes, of course you are, but hear me out, because—sorry to be a killjoy—time is shorter than you think. I'm not saying you should have children if you don't want to have them. In fact, if you don't want to have them, please don't. Most parents would kill to have grandchildren at some point, but that's not your problem; it's theirs. If, however, you are even the slightest bit interested in having a child or children one day, then biology, fertility, and logic—and the accumulation of sobering data on the risks of advanced maternal and paternal age on the genetics of a developing fetus—should compel you to do so before the age of thirty-five. Yes, both men and women can now freeze their gametes for later, and that can help widen the fertility window. But nothing changes the laws of gravity nor lessens its wear and tear on the aging knee, which will not be pleased when you have to bend it to play on the floor with your offspring.

D is for Disappointment

None of us is immune to disappointment. Friends will disappoint you. Jobs and bosses will disappoint you. Test results and meals and supposedly good films will disappoint you. Lovers and spouses and relatives will disappoint you, if they haven't done so already, repeatedly. That promotion will be denied. The house of your dreams will go to a higher bidder. Your novel will sit unpublished in a drawer. The issue is not with the disappointment itself—that's part of life. The issue is how you deal with it. In fact, the secret to surviving disappointment is actually quite simple: Find yourself a refrigerator magnet with the words, "This, too, shall pass." Stare at it every time you reach for the carton of milk. Ponder its meaning when you discover the carton's empty. That should do the trick.

E is for Empathy

If you retain only one lesson from this book, let it be this: empathy is not an optional feature or an add-on; it is as integral to your life as the engine is to a car. Empathy is the lifeblood of relationships, the glue between lovers, the intangible force that makes us human. The *Oxford English Dictionary* defines empathy as "the ability to understand and share the feelings of another." This is not to be confused with sympathy, which is defined as "feelings of pity and sorrow for someone else's misfortune." The difference between the passive state of sympathy—*what a shame she has cancer*—and the more active state of empathy—*why don't I sit with you while you have chemo and then drive you home, or would it be more useful if I did your laundry?*—is like the difference between sleepwalking through life and living it with the full breadth of your heart and humanity.

F is for Funerals

When we talk about death, or really any time we gather together with other still-living people to mourn someone who has died, what we're actually talking about is life: the way we live; how we live; the stuff we do—not the stuff we accumulate—with the short time we're given. Even the funeral of an ogre can teach us something about how *not* to live. Also, please remember, a funeral is never for the person in the box. It's for those left behind. If a good friend has lost a loved one, you throw on some black and you go. If it's too far away, forget the flowers: send food. People always forget to cook and eat when they're mourning. Write a condolence card, to the best of your abilities, filled with heart and memory, but don't you dare say, "He's in a better place." Are you kidding? He's not. He's dead.

G is for Grooming

Perhaps this goes without saying, but cut your hair every six to twelve weeks. Cut your nails once a week. (Especially your toenails. Nothing is a bigger turnoff or menace in bed than talons for toenails.) Shower once a day. Wear deodorant to the office. If you must wear a scent, less is always more. None is better. After thirty, use a face cream, regardless of your gender. Your future skin will be grateful. Brush your teeth twice a day if not thrice; floss daily; and get your teeth cleaned twice a year. Death enters, as they say, through the gums. Anything else—makeup, shaving, plucking, etcetera—is up to your own taste and discretion.

H is for Happiness

Happiness is not a state to be sought after, like a gold star or a holy grail. It is the reward that you get when you stop trying to find it. Pause for a moment. Listen to your own breath. Put on some music. Watch a baby sleep. Stare at a flower. Go for a walk. Reach for your lover's hand. There. That's happiness. It isn't anything more complicated than that.

I is for Intoxication

You think no one saw the beer cans in the recycling bin when you were in high school? Or noticed that the vodka had been diluted with water? What about that flung-open bedroom window? It was just stuffy inside, you say? Please. Few of us make it through our teen years without a drink or a toke, and these habits often follow us into adulthood, sometimes with damaging results. Here's the thing: as you grow older, the aftereffects of drugs and alcohol become harder to handle. At the same time, social interactions without the crutch of social lubricant become easier. But don't wait until you're an old fart to alter the paradigm. Try an experiment right now (or next weekend, or whenever you're brave enough): Go to one party—just one—and stay sober. Be truthful. Get real. You might have the kind of exchange with another human that blows your mind, naturally.

J is for Jung

Carl Jung, father of five, said, "Children are educated by what the grown-up is and not by his talk," so you might want to take everything he says with a grain of salt. But do please read him, sooner rather than later. In fact, now is the perfect time. Your mind is open to life's contradictions, absurdities, and heretofore unnoticed connections, which you may not have understood until you left home and realized the fallibility not only of your parents but of every adult ever ensured with your education, health, and welfare. Read Jung and you will learn not only to think for yourself but also to perceive and articulate a great deal more about society at large and about the masks we so often wear to survive it. Think of it this way: you must know your mask in order to remove it.

K is for Kitchen

Learn how to cook. Instant ramen is not cooking. Micro-
wave popcorn is not cooking. Going out to eat is expensive.
Teach yourself the basics beyond pasta with butter. It's not
hard. In fact, some people find cooking to be relaxing—even
meditative—especially after a long day at the office. Most
delicious things start with the simplest ingredients, such
as onions and garlic sautéed in olive oil. Find recipes for the
dishes you enjoy and spend a little time learning to cook
them. Then feed them to your friends and see how great it
feels to nourish people you love. Speaking of which . . .

L is for Love

This is your purpose here: to love and be loved. Full stop. Life is meaningless without it. It doesn't have to be romantic love, although romantic love, as you might already be well aware, can be the most wonderful love of all. It can also be the most painful. Sorry. You can't have one without the risk of the other. And just because it ends doesn't mean it never existed. Even the worst marriages begin with a dollop of love and good intentions. Love everyone you can: the people who live next door and also the door next to theirs. Love your friends. Love the little old lady in the street and the beggar on the corner and the grumpy guy filling your coffee order and the author of the book that made you cry. Love with abandon when you can, cautiously when you must, freely always. Love your life, even when it feels unlivable. It's the only one you've got.

M is for Mortgage

Many well-meaning people will tell you that you cannot consider yourself an adult until you have a mortgage. This is crazy talk. Of course, having a mortgage often makes fiscal sense, but sometimes renting is the better option. It depends upon where you are in life: how mobile you want to be, your income, your goals, your marital status, and your tolerance for uncertainty. Larger forces, like the economy, interest rates, and cost of living also come into play. At any rate, a mortgage no more makes you an adult than not having one makes you a child. You are not your stuff, you are not your money, you are not your job, you are not your home, and you are most certainly not your mortgage. Ownership is a collective illusion, a social agreement, and the people with the most stuff at the end of life do not win. They just disappear. Like all of us.

N is for No

Be as open as you can to saying yes in life, but learn to say no, too, when necessary. You do not have unlimited time or resources. You cannot help out every stranger, friend of a friend, or even friend who asks. You are not obligated to have sex when you don't feel like it. You do not have to go to your in-laws' for the holidays just because they want you to. (Do visit them, but do it when you'll actually enjoy the visit, not out of a sense of obligation during peak-season travel.) Turn down an assignment at work if it means missing your kid's school play or your spouse's birthday, or if a family medical emergency arises. If you get fired for saying no under these circumstances, then that company was not one for which you wanted to work in the first place.

O is for Offline

Whatever you're searching for, it's not in Google. Turn off your phone. Shut down your computer. Get out into nature and go for a walk. Notice your body, the way it takes up space. Stare into space. Look at the stars. Read a book. Paint a picture. Go to a museum. Do yoga. Cry. Dance. Laugh. Which brings us to . . .

P is for Play

"You can discover more about a person in an hour of play than in a year of conversation," said Plato. Play, for an adult, can be just about anything that unleashes your inner child. Moreover, scientists are now finding evidence of its importance to our well-being. Play is critical not only for keeping depression at bay but also for powering our brains to make the kinds of incongruous connections that lead to art, innovation, job success, and personal growth. This is not about competitive sports—though if that frees your child brain, knock yourself out. It's more about acting goofy: taking an improv class, giggling, ice skating, dancing naked, playing charades, throwing a Frisbee, riding a bike. The list is endless. Add to it.

Q is for "Quality over Quantity"

Always keep this phrase in the back of your head, like a fortune cookie mantra folded into your psyche. It won't apply in every situation, but it will apply in many. Would you rather have three scratchy sweaters that will fall apart by next winter, or one really soft cashmere one that will last several decades? Would you rather gorge on an entire bag of mass-produced treats, or enjoy one great, handcrafted chocolate truffle? Would you rather spend your weekend running from here to there, always late for the next thing, or calmly planted in one place, soaking up the experience? Would you rather watch seventy-five cat videos or *The 400 Blows*? And please don't say you haven't seen *The 400 Blows*. What are you waiting for? It's one of the greatest films of all time. Watch it right now.

R is for Risk

"Nothing ventured, nothing gained" has been around since Chaucer, but just because it's become a cliché doesn't mean it's not still as true today as it was in Middle English. In just about every realm of your life—love and work, in particular—you must take risks. Yes, you might speak your love out loud and have it not reciprocated, or you might try to cure cancer and fail. You might go on fifty dates that suck or create a film the world deems unwatchable. But you can't reach the summit of Mount Everest, kids, until you've stumbled over a whole mountainside of rocks and ice. As a professor of mine once told a lecture hall full of photojournalist wannabes, "A good photographer is never afraid of death. He seeks it out; he gets close enough to smell it. He lives every single one of his days as if it were his last. Otherwise, his pictures are shit." This is an extreme version of risk—I'm not suggesting here that you run off to be a war photographer—but it gets at the gist of it.

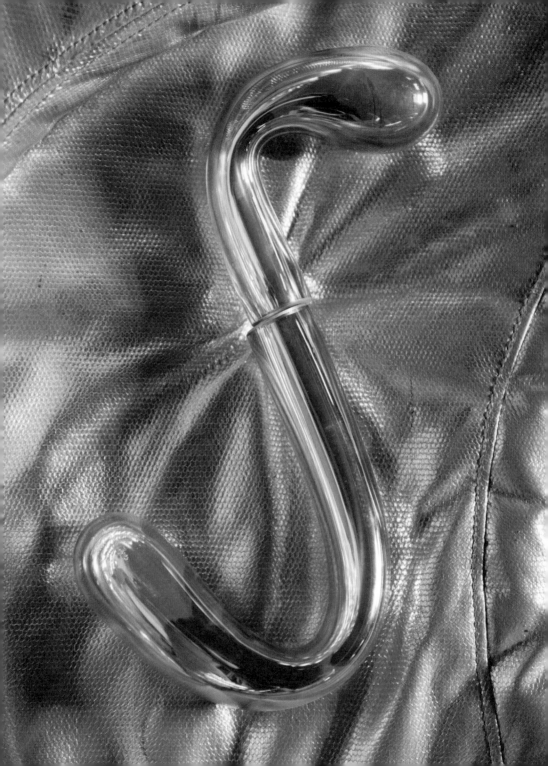

S is for Sex

You do not, contrary to what you might have heard in health class, have to be in love with someone to have sex with them. You should, however, at least like them enough to share an experience of such intimacy. Once you find a willing partner who fits this description, by all means, go for it. Have sex as often as you like. It's one of life's greatest pleasures, and don't let any scold tell you otherwise. Remove shame from the bedroom altogether, if you can. Love your body with all its beautiful flaws. Keep the light on. Explore parts of yourself you might normally keep hidden. Take several minutes to really stare into your lover's eyes. Give as well as you receive; receive as well as you give. Slow it down. Speed it up. Vary the tone depending on how you feel. "Everything is about sex," a wise shrink once told me, "except for sex, which is about aggression." Chew on that (while gently nibbling on your lover's ear).

T is for Tolerance

If you haven't noticed by now, the worst things on earth are fueled by intolerance, with war sitting at the tippy top of that list. You have not only to allow for the imperfections and differences of others but also to accept them without judgment. We're talking both macro and micro here, both at home with friends and family and in the world at large. Tolerate flaws in your spouse and parents, so long as they don't cause you harm. Be tolerant of who others actually are instead of dwelling on who you'd like them to be. Tolerate opinions, lifestyles, gender identifications, modalities, and skin tones that differ from yours. Judgment is easy; tolerance is hard. Work at it.

U is for Underwear

Cotton. Many pairs. No holes. Always clean. This is one of those instances where "quality over quantity" does not exactly hold true. Underwear wears out quickly, no matter the cost, and time between laundry days is precious, so find the best cotton you can in a style you like at the most reasonable price and buy twenty. Whether you're at home or on the road, an extra pair of underwear will always serve you well. Expensive lingerie and silk boxers are their own universe. If you're into that and want to spend your money and time hand-washing them, by all means, go for it.

V is for Vulnerability

When you were born, you were about as vulnerable as any living creature can be. You couldn't feed yourself. You couldn't care for yourself. Your neck was too weak to hold up your head, and your legs were of no use whatsoever in getting you from here to there. If your parents had left you alone in the forest back then, you'd be a goner, and they'd be in jail. Your job as a child was to transcend that vulnerability, to learn how to navigate in and out of the forest on your own. But hold that thought, Hansel and Gretel, because get this: your job as an adult is to reverse that progress. Now that you're big and strong and out in the world, you must learn not only to tap into that vulnerability and weakness within yourself but also to share it with others. True connection is impossible if you don't let down your guard. So shed a tear. Hug a stranger. Belt out that karaoke version of Nina Simone's "Feeling Good" without worrying if you're in tune. It's okay. No one in the karaoke bar is ever really in tune. We're all just humming along, doing the best we can, stumbling our way through this dark and scary forest together.

W is for Work

If there's one thing adults can get really confused about, it's self-definition and work. One of the first things we often ask one another is "What do you do?" It's a way of breaking the ice, yes, but it also makes us categorize one another in ways that turn out to be absurd. If you're Julianne Moore working as a waitress while waiting for her big break, or Franz Kafka shuffling papers in an insurance company, calling yourself a waitress or an insurance broker has little bearing on who you are. Everyone needs to pay the bills, yes, but your job—one of the most important of your life—is to figure out what valuable service you can offer the universe that makes you lose track of time. That's it. The whole shebang. Some people call this *flow*. You can call it whatever you'd like. Don't worry if you don't find it right out of the gate. You may change careers and paths several times. You may become a hybrid of sorts: a doctor who sculpts; a schoolteacher who codes; a writer (ahem) who shoots photographs. Don't be afraid of this. In fact, be open to it. Also? Please don't get so caught up by work that you forget to take periodic breaks. It doesn't have to be expensive. Yes, exploring far off countries or relaxing on a beach are wonderful, but so is simply stepping outside your front door to discover a new street or visit a local tourist attraction you may have scoffed at. The point is to give your brain the time and space it needs to rejuvenate, wherever that time and space can be found.

X is for Xylophone

If you can teach yourself to play "Twinkle, Twinkle, Little Star" on a toy xylophone, you can teach yourself to play just about any instrument. Not all of us are talented in the music department, but everyone who plays an instrument will tell you what a gift it is to be able to play one, whether poorly or well. Plus it's never too late to learn. By the same token, anyone can pick up a paintbrush or write a story or build a model or shoot a short film or draw a doodle or do an interpretive dance to Led Zeppelin. Art is not reserved for professional artists. Make it part of your life.

Y is for Yesterday

Yesterday is in the past. Tomorrow is in the future. They don't matter. So stop stressing over them. Stress is terrible, not only on your body and psyche, but also on everyone in your orbit. You can't change the past, and you can't control the future. You can merely learn from the former and make hopeful plans for the latter, none of which may come to fruition. The only thing that matters—the only thing that is real—is this moment, right now. Live it.

Z is for Zzzzzzzz

A through Y are not possible without eight hours of Zs a night, kids. All the scientists say so. They also say not to use your computer or smartphone before bed: the light affects your ability to sleep. Turn on a lamp and pick up an old-fashioned book, with pages. Turn to your partner. Turn to yourself. Just be. So many of us underestimate the power of being. It's not doing nothing. It's everything.

Acknowledgments

Deborah wishes to thank . . . Jacob Kogan, whose imminent departure triggered his mother's labors herein; Justin McLeod, for writing the code that enabled the gametes of this book to meet; Randy Polumbo, for texting the ovarian doodle that metamorphosed into triplets; Michael Chabon, for making the *shidduch* with Christine Carswell; Christine Carswell, for her enthusiastic consent and virtual hugs, and to the rest of the Chronicle Books Midwives, especially Sara, Casie, Jen, Yolanda, and Steve; Sasha Kogan, for caring for her baby brother above and beyond the call of familial duty; Leo Kogan, for gamely schlepping along on his mother's hunting and gathering; Lisa Leshne, for sweeping the authors and this book off their feet; Randy Polumbo (again, always) for gleefully feeding the beast with photographic sustenance from Joshua Tree and beyond and for nurturing his coauthor with Emmylou Harris, sage, and wisdom; and finally to society and its institutions at large, for teaching us everything we need to know about the miracle of our existence, except how to be.

Randy also wishes to thank Michael Chabon, Lisa Leshne, Christine Carswell, and the Chronicle gang for all the aforementioned reasons, but also . . . Deborah Copaken, for starting the fire, tending it so ferociously and beautifully, and for making it easy and fun. Also thanks to Deb for being so positive, encouraging, and unabashedly creative in the kitchen, on the guitar, behind the lens, and with her mighty pen! Sarah and Richard Zacks, for owning both a house full of books and a bookstore, as well as for instilling the value of book learning; Sidney MacKenzie and John Fulop, for adopting this kid into their young adult New York fold; Mrs. Susan Kaplan, for being the badassest high school AP English teacher in Providence, Rhode Island and for unleashing the alphabet into an improvisational and expressionistic froth! and finally to Nico LeMoal-Polumbo, for making this topic so inspiring and fascinating, and for teaching everyone in her orbit that L is for Love has no boundaries.